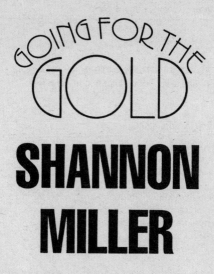

GOING FOR THE GOLD

SHANNON MILLER

SEPTIMA GREEN

AN AVON CAMELOT BOOK

GOING FOR THE GOLD: SHANNON MILLER is an original publication of Avon Books. This work has never before appeared in book form.

AVON BOOKS
A division of
The Hearst Corporation
1350 Avenue of the Americas
New York, New York 10019

Copyright © 1996 by Septima Green
Published by arrangement with the author
Library of Congress Catalog Card Number: 96-4130
ISBN: 0-380-78680-X
RL: 4.9

Library of Congress Cataloging in Publication Data:
Green, Septima.
   Going for the gold : Shannon Miller / Septima Green.
       p.   cm.
Summary: Examines the life of the highly decorated gymnast.
1. Miller, Shannon, 1977– —Juvenile literature. 2. Gymnasts—United States—Biography—Juvenile literature. [1. Miller, Shannon, 1977– . 2. Gymnasts.] I. Title.
GV460.2.M55G74   1996   96-4130
796.44'092—dc20   CIP
[B]   AC

First Avon Camelot Printing: June 1996

CAMELOT TRADEMARK REG. U.S. PAT. OFF. AND IN OTHER COUNTRIES, MARCA REGISTRADA, HECHO EN U.S.A.

Printed in the U.S.A.

OPM   10   9   8   7   6   5   4   3   2

Dedicated to the memory of
Shauna Renee Cook
October 14, 1983–September 25, 1994

Acknowledgments

Thanks to the many friendly, helpful people I encountered in Edmond, Oklahoma. People at Edmond North High, Summit Middle, and Charles Haskell Elementary schools were all especially courteous—not just those I interviewed, but the entire office staffs, who gave me time and cheerfully answered all my follow-up calls. Kim Henry, Tessa Miller, and Ed Livermore also deserve special thanks. Paul Ziert and his staff at *International Gymnast* magazine, plus the staff at *USA Gymnastics* magazine, aided in my research numerous times. Finally, though she was a distance away, I could not have completed this project without the support of Nonie Green.

Contents

1

Five Olympic Medals

As the United States flag was raised, four feet seven inch tall, seventy-one pound Shannon Miller stood on the awards podium in Barcelona, Spain. She had just won an Olympic bronze medal for the women's gymnastic floor exercise. Hundreds of television cameras captured the fifteen-year-old girl smiling and waving to the standing-room-only crowd. Because this was her fifth medal in the Games, the audience reacted warmly to the familiar figure on the podium. They stood and cheered boisterously for her.

Shannon proved you can be small and still

win big. She was the tiniest U.S. athlete in any sport, yet earned more medals than any other American in either the winter or summer Olympic Games of 1992. No other female gymnast from any country participating in the Olympics won five medals.

It all began on Sunday, July 26, when Shannon and ninety-one other women from twenty-four countries began their quest for Olympic medals in gymnastics. Each country sends its best, and even though some individuals and teams are seeded higher than others, the competition is unpredictable. In gymnastics, there is no finish line and no indisputable winner. Judges use a Code of Points to score the events, but they sometimes favor the one who pleases them the most.

The United States Olympic Committee expected Shannon to do well; but 1991 world and three-time national champion Kim Zmeskal was touted as the USA's star. Kim appeared on the covers of *Time* magazine and *TV Guide* prior to Barcelona. Other USA team participants were

Wendy Bruce, Dominique Dawes, Betty Okino, and Kerri Strug.

Gymnasts can win Olympic medals in three categories. Each contains the events of vault, uneven bars, balance beam, and floor exercise. A perfect score on any event is 10.00, but the women begin each routine with a 9.4, to which judges may add or subtract points during the performance. The first category is Team Competition, which includes *compulsories,* routines that have specific movements required of all participants, and *optionals,* different routines creatively designed by the individual gymnasts.

Shannon, who had made a miraculous comeback from elbow surgery four months before, began compulsories by scoring a 9.912 on the bars. Her beam and floor routines drew a 9.887 each, and she nailed her vault for the highest score in the event, a 9.95. Her total of 39.636 topped all the other gymnasts in the world! Shannon and Steve Nunno, her coach, already knew how seriously she took her sport. Now the rest of the world did, too.

Shannon knew not to be too dazed by her

outstanding performances. She needed to concentrate on her optional routines. Her ability to stay calm and confident makes her a good competitor. This time, she earned a total of 39.675, giving her a grand total of 79.311—the highest individual score in the team competition.

The entire U.S. team did well—so well, that they won the team bronze medal! The Unified Team (formerly the Soviet Union) took the gold, and Romania took the silver. But only a small margin separated the three team medal-winning countries.

Wearing their red, white, and blue warm-up suits with "USA" in eight-inch-high letters across the front of their jackets, the team lined up on the podium in the order of Betty, Wendy, Dominique, Shannon, Kerri, and Kim. Each held a bouquet of flowers high above her head. Their smiles were as bright as the precious new medals that hung around their necks. Shannon said that for her, standing on the awards podium with her teammates was one of the best parts of the Olympic Games.

The most coveted medal category is the All-

Around. The thirty-six highest-scoring women in team competition advance to these finals, but no country can have more than three representatives. Gymnasts, assigned to squads, or groups, enter a new round of competition as they make rotations to each apparatus (piece of gymnastics equipment) area, where they perform one optional routine. Because the events happen simultaneously, spectators often feel that they're viewing a four-ring circus! The gymnast who earns the greatest point total from all events earns the gold.

Fortunately, the gymnasts had a day off between team and all-around competition. Shannon spent most of the day working out and polishing her routines.

Then, on Thursday, July 30, the expectant crowd at the Montjuic Stadium in Barcelona witnessed the closest all-around contest in Olympic history. It happened that Shannon Miller and Ukrainian Tatiana Gutsu were placed on the same squad. Both girls performed at a high level of difficulty on each apparatus. Everytime their scores were incredibly close.

They kept the audience in suspense. Shannon's quiet nature concealed the pressure she felt. Finally, on the vault, she sprinted down the runway with perfect form and landing. The crowd shouted that she deserved a 10.00, but the judges awarded her a 9.975. Tatiana's second vault, a 9.95, allowed her to slip past Shannon's total score by 0.012.

The three Romanian all-around finalists and former Olympic medalist Svetlana Boginskaya of Belarus gave Tatiana and Shannon some close competition, but not enough. Tatiana won the gold, and Shannon won the silver. Shannon's all-around silver is the first all-around medal of any kind won by an American in a nonboycotted Olympics.

The third category in which one can earn medals is Individual Finals. The top eight finishers in each event from the team competition qualify. Each country may have no more than two competitors per event. Of the ninety-two hopefuls in Barcelona, only Shannon and Lavinia Milosovici of Romania qualified in all events.

Once again Shannon made Olympic history, because no other American has ever qualified for all four individual apparatus finals. By this time, the demands and pressures were beginning to take their toll on the athletes. Shannon wasn't about to give in to fatigue or the fact that she had four more major routines to perform. She readied herself both mentally and physically. She treated each event as though it were her only chance to perform. She gracefully, yet powerfully, delivered the near perfection the audience had come to expect from her. Shannon isn't a bubbly type like Mary Lou Retton, but crowds love her artistic quality and the way she draws them into her performance.

She dominated the competition, winning three out of a possible four medals. She tied for the silver on the beam and took the bronze for bars and floor exercise. Lavinia Milosovici won the gold for her perfect floor routine and a silver for her vault, but Shannon's total results were 0.524 higher. Tatiana Gutsu earned one silver and one bronze.

At the end of the week, Shannon had outscored every other gymnast in the team and individual categories. The only time she slipped to second was for the oh-so-close all-around medal.

"Is that history or what?" exclaimed Coach Steve Nunno. "This little girl walks off with a fistful of medals. Flawless. Not one major mistake in the entire Games."

Shannon, too, felt proud of her accomplishments. "I was going for the gold, definitely, but I'm really happy with all my medals. I did my best. It feels great. It feels better than I ever expected it to be," she said.

Before Barcelona, people in Edmond, Oklahoma, and in gymnastic circles knew of Shannon Miller. By the end of the Olympic Games of 1992, the USA's star athlete became a household name.

2

Shannon and Tessa
Get a Trampoline

Her name held no special significance, say Ron and Claudia Miller. Dr. Miller laughs when asked about his second daughter's name. ''Claudia suggested all sorts of girls' names, but I picked Shannon because it was the only one I'd heard before!

''Living in Rolla, Missouri, at the time, I also accepted the name because I knew of Mike Shannon, a St. Louis Cardinals baseball sportscaster.

''We chose my mother's middle name of Lee, because Shannon and Lee sounded good together,'' Dr. Miller continues.

9

Recently an Irish fan wrote that the two main rivers in Ireland are the Shannon and the Lee. From a family standpoint, it seems that, indeed, Shannon Lee Miller's name is appropriate. Claudia's father is Irish and her mother is half Irish and half Mexican, and Ron's mother is Irish.

All four grandparents still live in San Antonio, Texas, the city where Ron and Claudia grew up and met when they attended Trinity University in the late 1960s.

When Shannon was born on March 10, 1977, the Millers' older daughter, Tessa, was nearly two. Ron Miller had earned his doctorate at the University of Missouri the year before, and in the summer of 1977 he began teaching at Central State University (now called the University of Central Oklahoma). Shannon was four months old when she moved with her family to Edmond, Oklahoma. Located adjacent to Oklahoma City, Edmond has a population of 65,000.

Shannon was independent even as a toddler. When she was eighteen months old, she gave her mother a real scare. Claudia Miller and her two small daughters were in J. C. Penney's baby department at Shepherd Mall. Claudia saw her girls go around the corner of a table of baby clothes. When she looked up a minute or two later, she saw Tessa, but not Shannon. She asked Tessa where Shannon was, and Tessa said she didn't know. Mrs. Miller looked all around and began asking people, "Have you seen a blond, curly-haired girl?" No one had. She began to panic because the entrance to the mall was close by. Mrs. Miller and Tessa ran through the store crying and grabbing people to ask if they'd seen Shannon.

Finally a tall, older gentleman calmly said to come with him. He directed them to the shoe department where, behind the counter, little Shannon was trying on a pair of men's big black shoes! Mrs. Miller said it's funny to look back on it. "And," she said, "it's ironic because to this day, Shannon has a shoe fetish. You can't take her into a mall without her looking at shoes. That kid's got a closet full of shoes!"

Another time, Mrs. Miller and Tessa planned a shopping trip that didn't include Shannon.

Shannon got really upset, so her father said he'd take her on a motorcycle ride. Only two years old, she seemed satisfied. "Okay, Tessa gets to go with Mom, but I get to ride on the motorcycle with Dad!"

Dr. Miller thought she'd be exceedingly scared. He sat her up on the gas tank and told her where to hold on. "I thought she'd probably get a death-grip on those handles," he explained. "We'd gone about 200 yards when she spotted a cat three houses ahead."

"Kitty cat," Shannon said as she pointed to it and laughed.

"There she was, balanced on that gas tank, totally unafraid!" her dad recalls.

It seems that Shannon performed quite a few tricks in her early years. The couple who baby-sat for her later confessed to a "game" Shannon liked to play. Larry would put Shannon on top of the refrigerator. She would jump off and he would catch her.

Another early example of Shannon's independent spirit was the time Ron Miller's brother, who was attending school in Indiana, stopped in Edmond on his way to San Antonio for Christmas. The Miller family also planned to go to San Antonio. Shannon, less than three years old, decided her Uncle Roger needed company, and the two of them rode all the way to San Antonio together.

That year the Miller girls received a jungle gym. Tessa says she and Shannon called it the "tug boat." Tessa remembers, "It had a wire frame with white and blue metal bars connected box-style. There were flat bars on the bottom where you could stand or sit. We played on it a lot and sometimes got to take our lunch out and eat on the tug boat."

Twelve days before Christmas 1980, Shannon and Tessa welcomed their new baby brother, Troy. "We were too young to be excited. It was like any other Christmas," Tessa says, "except the tree was in the dining room instead of the study."

Shannon was four and a half when one of her toys ended up on the neighbor's roof. John, the neighbor, lifted her high enough to crawl up and get the toy. Then, getting off the roof seemed to be a problem. John said, "Jump, I'll catch you!"

Dr. Miller remembers thinking, "She won't jump off trusting someone she barely knows to catch her." But she did.

Of all the toys or gifts Shannon received as a child, she and her family best remember the trampoline Santa Claus brought in 1981. Shannon told her parents she was getting a trampoline for Christmas because she had asked Santa. That was it. She was sure the trampoline would be there. Claudia Miller realized their daughter really expected a trampoline. She knew they were expensive and could be dangerous. She says, "As the time drew closer, we decided we were going to have one very disappointed kid on our hands if Shannon didn't get a trampoline." They saw an ad for a used one that was in really good shape. Claudia's mother paid for part of it so they could afford it.

Some friends kept it in their garage until Christmas Eve and brought it over after the girls had gone to bed. On Christmas morning, despite a temperature of nine degrees and a 25 mile-per-hour wind, Ron and Claudia's brother set it up in the backyard because Shannon wanted to "jump on it *now*." Sure enough, in spite of the bitterly cold weather, Shannon and Tessa went out for a few minutes to jump on their trampoline.

This was the first of two trampolines the Millers eventually owned. Their three children, plus a host of neighborhood kids, received hours of pleasure jumping and tumbling on the trampolines.

Little Shannon Lee Miller jumped off refrigerators, roofs, and trampolines. What would be next?

3

Grade School and Gymnastics

Shannon and Tessa bounced on their trampoline so much that Claudia Miller enrolled them in a local gymnastics club. Soon afterwards, five-year-old Shannon and her gym club prepared to march in the Fourth of July parade. Shannon was excited because she would get to perform one of her favorite skills. In 1982, people in Edmond watched the tiny tot do back walkovers, unaware of the fame she would bring to their city ten years later.

In first grade, Shannon faced an indirect kind of competition—with her sister! Barbara Tabor taught both Miller girls. Shannon, academically talented and practically a "straight-A" student throughout her school career, didn't measure up to her sister's perfect record. When Tessa was in Ms. Tabor's room, she read *Treasure Island, Black Beauty,* and other novels for older kids. Shannon, instead of treating the situation as a negative, tried to live up to the standard Tessa set. She says it wasn't easy following Tessa, but her sister's example made her work harder to try to get As.

Charles Haskell Elementary was a brand-new building when it opened its doors for Shannon's second-grade year. Shannon and Tessa rode the bus each day, but they didn't always sit together. One day Tessa got off and walked home. Her dad asked where Shannon was. Tessa assumed she had gotten off on the second stop close to their house. After a few minutes, Ron Miller called the school. Pretty soon the bus brought Shannon home. She had fallen asleep on one of the backseats. She was so small that the driver didn't see her until he'd driven the bus back to the bus barn!

The girls didn't have to ride the bus much

longer because they and some other girls from gym club formed a car pool. When they didn't have gym, Ron Miller picked them up between his classes.

That year, Shannon's coach realized she had special talent and suggested that she take the USAIGC (United States Association of Independent Gymnastic Clubs) test. If a gymnast passes, she gets to go to a camp to learn new skills and work out with other higher level gymnasts. Claudia Miller drove Shannon to Waco, Texas, to take the test. Two other girls took the test with Shannon. They knew in advance what was on the test and passed. Shannon's coach hadn't prepared her, but she watched the other girls and tried to do what they did. Gary, the examiner, asked Shannon to do skills of which she had no knowledge. After working with her, he determined that she had potential and recommended that she learn more skills and come back in six months to take the test again. One of the skills Gary said she could practice at home was a pressed handstand.

Shannon could do regular handstands or

headstands easily, but this pressed handstand frustrated her. She had to begin the move with her hands and feet on the floor, legs apart, and slowly press herself up to a handstand position. A gymnast has to practice the skill to develop the strength required to perform it. Shannon couldn't seem to make herself practice this particular move.

About this time, Cabbage Patch Dolls came to Oklahoma City. Shannon really wanted one of those dolls. Her parents told her, "You master the pressed handstand, then we'll get you a Cabbage Patch Doll." Within a week, she had her doll.

In addition to playing with their dolls, Shannon and Tessa used to create "houses" within their shared bedroom or sometimes downstairs. The girls connected blankets from their desk to the bed and made little hideaway tents. Sometimes they put on makeup and played "beauty." Once Shannon cut and styled Tessa's hair. Tessa says Shannon had a good sense of style as young as seven or eight.

One time the Miller girls dressed as nerds.

They put on huge, wildly colored shirts. Shannon wrapped injury tape around Tessa's glasses and wore them. Tessa put on one of their dad's ties. Their silly behavior and attire put their parents in stitches.

Shannon and Tessa enjoyed going to their dad's university after school. "Troy wasn't in school yet. He had a regular baby-sitter. It was like Shannon and I were special. We were *big* girls," Tessa says. After school, their dad let them stay in a lab that wasn't being used. They took their blankets, made their tent houses, and then watched *The Price Is Right,* other game shows, and sitcoms on TV.

"All of my memories with Shannon are good," says Tessa. "But these were the best times—the times before she became Shannon the gymnast, and she was just Shannon my sister."

4

Shannon Meets Steve Nunno

A major turning point on the road to becoming "Shannon the gymnast" occurred during the summer after Shannon finished third grade. Her gym club planned a two-week trip to the Soviet Union. Shannon could hardly wait for the trip to begin. She had traveled to nearby states before, but never out of the country.

To earn money for the trip, her club put on exhibitions. When a local television station covered the story, a reporter asked Shannon, "If the Russians teach you to become better gymnasts, what are you going to teach them?"

"To boogie!" she replied.

It turned out that the young Edmond gymnasts worked with coaches in Moscow, Russia, at the same gym where Steve Nunno was attending a seminar to learn the Soviet coaching system. Steve Nunno, then an elite coach in Norman, Oklahoma, and about to open his own gym in Oklahoma City, saw the small recreational group and felt embarrassed. He said the Russians expected to see high-level U.S. athletes. Instead they saw this low-level group just having fun. He saw the Russians offering the U.S. gymnasts skills that were way above their ability.

"I noticed this one girl, Shannon Miller, trying her very hardest to do these high-level skills, and she was actually upset that she couldn't do them," Mr. Nunno says. "It was funny to me that she really thought she was going to do this double layout and these double backs that the coaches were literally throwing her through." Steve Nunno became intrigued with the idea that if he could channel her frustration, he could help her learn to do those kinds of big skills.

In Russia, the coaches recommended that

Shannon take up high-level gymnastics. Later that summer, Claudia Miller called Steve Nunno to ask if Shannon could try out for his newly formed Dynamo team in Oklahoma City. Coach Nunno accepted her, and at age nine, Shannon's competitive training began.

When Shannon returned to Haskell Elementary that fall, she paid a visit to her third-grade teacher and presented her with a box of Russian pencils. Susan Hall still has the pencils in their box, which bears the label *Kohetpyktop*. Ms. Hall says, ''Shannon was quiet and shy in my class, and very responsible.'' At first, Shannon's elementary teachers worried about her missing school and spending so many hours doing gymnastics. They thought gym interfered with her academics, but they later discovered that her grades were always among the best in the class.

Shannon also remembered to bring Kim Henry a souvenir from Russia. Kim and Shannon met as second-grade classmates. In elementary school the two friends were about the same size, always the smallest in their class. Blond, hazel-eyed Shannon and brunette, brown-eyed Kim shared, among other things, an enthusiasm for gymnastics. Kim took lessons from Steve Nunno, but she was in a different group than Shannon.

At school when their teacher said, "It's time for recess," Shannon and Kim sprinted across the playground to get first "dibs" on the swings. They performed acrobatics on the swings and swung as high as possible. After swinging, they did tricks on the jungle gym. Then Kim led Shannon and their other friends in somersaults and cartwheels, and Shannon took the lead in doing back flips and round offs. All too soon the period ended. Back in the class-room, Shannon and Kim took their studies as seriously as they did their recess. Both girls made straight As.

A popular annual event at Haskell was the talent show. P.E. teacher June Coleman directed it. Due to the school's large enrollment and numerous talented children, participants in the show had to audition to secure a spot in the program. Shannon tried out in second and third and performed gymnastics routines. But in fourth grade she tried out and didn't make the show. Ms. Coleman said Shannon either didn't try hard enough or maybe she really didn't want to be in it. Ron and Claudia Miller were surprised their daughter wasn't chosen, but they were supportive of the judges' decision. Shannon's act for her fifth-grade year made the show and drew a big round of applause.

On Track and Field Day each spring, the students always looked forward to Shannon's high jump. She performed a gym flip over the bar unlike anyone else's.

June Coleman taught a mini-Olympics unit as part of the P.E. curriculum. As a culminating activity, parents came to watch the various "Olympic" events. Shannon and her gymnastic group from Steve Nunno's gym provided routines for the Opening Ceremony, causing spectators to ooh, ahh, and shout, "Bravo!"

Another Coleman P.E. unit was six weeks of gymnastics. When Ms. Coleman taught a forward roll, Shannon did a forward roll. She did exactly what the others did. Ms. Coleman said all of the kids admired Shannon for her talent, but her modest demeanor gained additional respect.

Shannon had good rapport with adults, too. One memorable incident happened near the end of the fifth-grade square dance program. They were about to dance the Virginia Reel, and the kids in the program went out into the audience to get a student or someone for a partner. Shannon picked Bill Nowell, the principal! Bill Nowell stood six feet three inches and Shannon stood four feet four inches. As dance partners, the contrast of his height with her tiny size was quite a sight!

At Charles Haskell School, an autographed, poster-size picture of Shannon is still exhibited.

5

Summit Middle School

Located across the large parking lot from Haskell Elementary, Summit Middle School sprawls out like a college campus. The two schools, built in a secluded location, are barely visible from the main street.

The beautiful country surroundings provided Shannon with an ideal place to receive an education. When she attended Summit from 1989–1991, she saw cows grazing in the fields next to the campus.

Every morning Shannon worked out at Steve Nunno's gym. Since classes had already started by the time she got to school, Shannon had to go by the office to sign in. Each day Summit's attendance clerk, Nancy Nelson, gave her an "admit slip." Finally one day, Ms. Nelson said, "Shannon, I've been signing all these slips for you. Will you sign something for me? When you're famous, I want to show it to my friends."

"Sure, I'd be glad to." She smiled and wrote, "Best wishes, Shannon Miller."

Before their seventh-grade year started, Shannon and Kim Henry devised a plan to help Shannon keep up with her schoolwork. Kim registered six class periods for herself, then Shannon fit her schedule to Kim's. That way, when Shannon had to go out of town for competitions, Kim took down all the assignments. Even their lockers were close by, Kim's located directly above Shannon's.

In order to have more time for other interests, Kim quit gymnastics in sixth grade. But she and Shannon still made their rounds in the shopping mall. They usually stopped at the White Mountain Ice Cream Shop (yogurt for Shannon), looked at clothes and shoes, and went to movies.

Kim gave Shannon a broken heart necklace

that said, "Best Friends." Each girl wore half of the heart. They still jumped on the trampoline at the Millers', although they used it less than they did in elementary school. Kim called Shannon "Miller" as a kind of nickname. There was a period when the girls were into *Winnie the Pooh,* and they would pass the time relating their friends to the different characters. Swimming occupied any spare time they had in the summer, but Shannon discovered she had less and less leisure time.

Consistently, people who know her say that Shannon is a master of time management. Schoolwork and remaining in public schools always have been priorities for her.

Zoe Baxter, her science teacher, says, "Sometimes she was gone for a whole week, and Shannon did every bit of work that she missed. I thought it was unusual for a seventh-grader to be that focused."

Ms. Baxter mentions that Shannon never bragged. When she returned from a competition, she didn't say, "I won this meet" or "I got this medal." Once in the teacher's lounge, Ms.

Baxter saw a national gymnastics magazine with Shannon's picture. She was pleased and surprised. "It was then that I knew she must be really good," says Ms. Baxter.

Steve Bowlware remembers that Shannon was a perfectionist in his honors math class. He was sympathetic to the fact that her competitive training in gymnastics caused her to miss a lot of school. He told her, "Look, Shannon, as long as I know you understand the concepts, you can do half of the work."

Shannon said, "Thank you, Mr. Bowlware." However, she came back with every single problem correctly worked.

Shannon was a math whiz, but she rarely spoke up in class. One way Mr. Bowlware got her to participate was to play the game "Simon Says" connected to math. Shannon, because of her ability to concentrate well, won every time. Another activity Shannon enjoyed was singing math formula songs.

To help students understand reciprocals in fractions, Steve Bowlware asked Shannon to stand on her hands. She did. "She stood straight up and down without moving a muscle for five minutes at least,'' Mr. Bowlware said. ''When she finally stood up, the kids said, 'More! More!' ''

Even though Shannon was shy, she had a lot of friends. Steve Bowlware had lunch duty during Shannon's lunch period. He observed her relating to various groups of kids. Her ability to interact well with any group impressed him.

Steve Bowlware says Shannon made a big impact on the school and students at Summit. Even though she spent more time doing gymnastics than anything else except sleeping, she maintained her straight-A report card and got along well with students and teachers.

6

Ambition and the Ascent

Gymnastics crept more and more into Shannon's life. No one had to force or coax her into it. She liked it from the beginning. After her Soviet Union trip, she thought competitive experiences would be fun. That's the reason she had transferred to Steve Nunno's gym.

As the time for her first competition drew near, Shannon began to have second thoughts about it. She talked with her grandmother, Mabel Lee Miller. "Grandma, I'm stressed."

"What's causing you to feel stressed?"

"I have to compete and I don't know how."

"Well, there was a time when you didn't know how to do gymnastics, wasn't there?"

"Yes, but I know now."

"That's what I mean. Your coaches will tell you what to do, and when the time comes for you to compete, you'll know how."

"Oh. Okay. But I'm still stressed!"

Shannon's first competition was in Dallas, Texas, November 29, 1986. She scored a respectable 30.45 in the optionals only, level 2 meet. The next week, in Kansas, she made a 33.4, finishing second to a girl from St. Louis, Missouri. The judges in Kansas thought Shannon was an experienced competitor. But at the Chalet in Norman, Oklahoma, two weeks later, Shannon got a 30.5 performing similar routines. The Oklahoma judges realized she was new, so they gave her more conservative scores. On a return trip to Kansas in February, she won first place with a 35.1. This competition had both compulsories and optionals, meaning Shannon had to do eight routines. She finally finished first in Oklahoma, in the town of Ardmore.

Most of Shannon's early competitions were

held within driving distance of Edmond. The first time she flew to her destination was in February 1987. Shannon's team was going to compete in Reno, Nevada. Her family took her to the airport. Ron Miller wondered if his fourth-grade daughter would cry, and wondered what he should tell her to make her feel calm and comfortable about the trip. But at the airport, instead of staying close by her parents, Shannon cheerfully said, "Good-bye," and marched over to join the older girls in her group.

In Reno, the team stayed at the Circus Casino, and they had to walk through the casino to get to their rooms. After they returned to Oklahoma, Steve Nunno looked seriously at the Millers and said, "I had to watch Shannon. She wanted to play the roulette table." Mr. Nunno was teasing, but Shannon did bring home some stuffed animals that a stranger won and handed to her.

These and numerous other local and regional meets taught Shannon what competition was all about. Mixed in with the glories, there were bouts of frustration. Like every gymnast, she sometimes fell from the apparatuses, not just in practice, but also in competition! If Shannon fell from the beam during competition, she began to play it safe, and when she did, her leaps weren't as high and her skills weren't executed as well. She discovered this conservative approach was getting her nowhere, and she finally realized that if she fell, that was the time to go all out. She learned that a good attitude and positive response to mistakes would help her win.

After each meet, Steve Nunno taught her how to make little corrections, and together they started to systematically improve her routines. He knew it wouldn't be long before Shannon would compete on national and international levels.

Nearly eleven years old in 1988, Shannon competed in the American Classic, Junior B, at Phoenix, Arizona. She felt happy when she placed second all-around at her first national meet. She was even happier at the U.S. Classic in Athens, Georgia, where she won first place all-around, plus first on vault and balance beam.

Ron and Claudia Miller wanted all of their

children to realize that if they happened to be good at something, "There's a larger world out there." They told Shannon, "Now you're good in gymnastics in Edmond, but there are girls all over the state training." Later they told her, "Now you're good in Oklahoma, but there are girls in Texas, Arizona, and Florida who are training. You'll need to keep working hard."

Coach Nunno wanted to see if Shannon could win international medals. She qualified for the 1988 Junior Pan-American Games in Ponce, Puerto Rico, where she won the all-around silver medal and a bronze on the uneven bars. She also helped the U.S. team win the team gold. "She made a couple of mistakes, but overall it was a great competition for Shannon," her coach recalls.

When gymnasts reach the point where they travel out of the country to competitions, expenses become a primary consideration. Gymnastics is not the most expensive sport. But the cost of the lessons can mount for Level 10 and Elite (the highest level) gymnasts, who require twenty to thirty-six hours of lessons and workouts per week. Girls need leotards, warm-up suits, grips, and music tapes for floor routines. Each meet has an entry fee. And travel expenses can really add up.

Ed Livermore, editor of *The Edmond Evening Sun,* points out that the Miller family made sacrifices to pay for Shannon's gymnastic expenses. He says, "Both parents work. They live in a nice house, but it's not a mansion on a hill. It's not like Ron Miller is the richest guy in town who lavished all the lessons on her. They sacrificed for her to be able to do this. No one handed the family or Shannon anything. And to me, it's the American ideal. Shannon Miller is the American story."

Tessa and Troy, proud as they are of their sister's success, are normal siblings who registered a few complaints along the way. Tessa was thirteen and Troy was seven on a particular visit to their Miller grandparents when they shared problems resulting from Shannon's gymnastics. Tessa said, "We don't have money to buy me name-brand clothes."

Then Troy said, "Yeah, we have to do Shannon's work sometimes, too."

Problems did occur as Shannon climbed to the top of the world in her sport. She and her family eventually solved them because they worked together and supported one another.

Continuing the climb, Shannon caught the attention of *International Gymnast* magazine writer and photographer Nancy Raymond in February 1989. The occasion was the Sixth Annual Dragon Invitational held at Kansas City Market Center. The regional meet hosted 115 competitors from eighteen Midwest gym clubs. Shannon placed eighth, but the style and execution of her routines impressed Nancy Raymond so much that she published a large picture of Shannon on the balance beam and detailed her routines for *International Gymnast* readers. This gave Shannon her first exposure in the popular magazine.

The following month, at the American Classic, Junior A, Shannon had her best national meet to date. There, in Oakland, California, she won four first places: all-around, bars, beam, and floor exercise.

Steve Nunno says one of his favorite competitions for Shannon was the July 1989 Olympic Sports Festival held at the Myriad Convention Center in Oklahoma City. Shannon delighted her hometown crowd of 11,000 as she won the gold medal on the bars and the bronze in the all-around. "Bela Karolyi expected his team of six to take all the medals, but Shannon broke up his six-pack," Mr. Nunno notes. "That's when I knew she was going to be a great competitor."

Shannon says, "It's hard to think of one favorite competition, but I'll always remember the Catania Cup in Italy." She and Agina Simpkins represented the United States, and Shannon became the first American ever to win the meet. She took home four gold trophies and one silver. "It was really neat to see the sights and spend some time in Rome after the competition," she adds.

In 1991, her second year on the U.S. senior national team, Shannon qualified for the world championship team. By now, she had competed in eleven international meets, but this was the big one! World championships carry as much prestige as the Olympics. However, some people rank the Olympics higher because they're only held every four years, and the worlds usually occur every year.

These championships took place in the United States in Indianapolis, Indiana. Shannon's mother and grandparents plus a few relatives who live in Indiana came to watch Shannon. They saw her place second in the world in compulsories and make the most points of anyone in the United States, which led the team to the silver medal. She also became the first American to qualify for all four apparatus event finals and won the silver medal on the uneven bars.

In December, Shannon and Scott Keswick became the crowd favorites in St. Gallen, Switzerland, where they won the Swiss Cup. Shannon's balance beam routine earned a perfect 10.00. Then, in Montreux, Switzerland, at the Arthur Gander Memorial competition, Shannon made her first gold sweep—meaning she won every possible event. Here she received another perfect 10.00 on the beam. Her combined score of 39.875 set a new record for this meet.

In 1992, Shannon had elbow surgery, which kept her from participating in the optional rounds of the USA Championships. She did, however, place first in compulsories. At the Olympic Trials in June, Shannon again placed first in compulsories. (Kim Zmeskal won optionals.) Both USA Championship and Olympic Trial scores count in determining who makes the team. Shannon and Kim's scores were exceedingly close, but Shannon won by a small fraction. The important thing was that she made the team.

As soon as the six members and one alternate are selected, the team trains together until time for the Olympics. Shannon could just imagine what her father's advice would be: "Now you're good in the United States, and you've won some international medals, but girls in Romania, Russia, and China are training. Keep working hard. There's a larger world out there."

7

Two Years on Top

The larger world out there became smaller for Shannon after she captured the silver all-around and four other Olympic medals. Before Shannon left the Olympic Village in Barcelona, NBC gymnastics commentator John Tesh made it possible for her to meet the USA's Dream Team. Shannon was thrilled to meet them and get their autographs. She was surprised to learn Magic Johnson wanted to meet her, too!

Returning to their respective homes in the United States, the Olympians stopped overnight in the nation's capital. President George Bush, senators, and other dignitaries met them at the White House and honored them with a reception at the Capitol. Shannon enjoyed the experiences made possible by her new status.

It felt like the world had come to Edmond to share in Shannon's triumphant return from Barcelona. Ron and Claudia Miller arrived home on Tuesday around midnight. They were due to meet Shannon's plane at noon the next day. After two eventful weeks abroad and having gotten to sleep at 2:00 A.M., Shannon's mom remembers, "It was hard to get up. We were *so-o* tired."

At the airport, they went around to the back and didn't see the huge crowd. When they did, they wondered, "What are all these people doing here? This is like a political convention." Of course, the people had come to welcome Shannon.

The Millers learned Edmond had planned a parade to honor their daughter. When they told her, Shannon said, "They're having a parade for just me? Isn't somebody else going to be in it?"

Claudia said, "I don't *think* so—it's just *you*."

"How could that be?"

"We don't *know!*"

The four-mile parade began off Memorial Road, south of downtown Edmond, and continued north on the Broadway Extension. The city closed the Broadway Extension, which is the most heavily traveled road in Oklahoma. Ron said, "It's 5:00 P.M. They're going to kill us [for holding up traffic]!"

Shannon sat up on the backseat of a convertible and smiled and waved to the people along the way. Ron, Claudia, Tessa, and Troy rode in a separate car. Coaches Steve Nunno and Peggy Liddick also rode in the parade.

There were signs everywhere: "Great job, Shannon!" "You're a perfect 10.00!" "We're proud of you!" Two helicopters flew overhead with trailing banners.

"We couldn't believe it. We couldn't fathom all the people. It blew my mind," Claudia says.

At the end of the parade, another surprise lay

in store for Shannon. The Saturn car dealership had opened in Oklahoma City not long before Shannon won her Olympic medals. Pat McConnell, finance manager of Saturn at the time, had the idea of giving Shannon a new car to use for a year. He and several other young men in charge of the dealership got owner Bob Moore's approval for the year's lease. "We had a lot of fun planning it," Mr. McConnell says. "We put all this together for Shannon in about three or four days."

Shannon and her family were standing on stage when Mr. McConnell drove the shiny red-and-silver sports coupe through the crowd. He got out, walked up on stage, and presented Shannon with a dozen red roses and the keys to the car. Shannon, already overwhelmed by the fabulous homecoming, could hardly believe all that was happening. This would be a day to remember!

Shannon later visited the Saturn dealership to attend a reception where Oklahoma Governor David Walters honored her. She signed autographs for gymnasts and other young people who wanted to meet her.

In addition to attending receptions and signing more autographs, Shannon received an unbelievable amount of mail. Over a thousand letters arrived within the first week after she returned home. People didn't need to know her complete address. The postal service delivered letters simply addressed: "Shannon Miller; Oklahoma City, Oklahoma" or "Shannon Miller; Edmond, Oklahoma." Prior to the Olympics, Shannon's volume of mail reached the point that Claudia asked the local postmaster, John Barmann, if any latitude could be given on the postage bill. Since there's no provision for persons of celebrity status to receive a postage discount, John Barmann spread the word at the local post office, where the employees passed the hat. They collected enough money to buy Shannon 1,000 first-class stamps!

When she first began to get fan mail, Shannon personally answered every letter. She says, "If someone out there cares enough to write, I want to answer." But it became a physical impossibility, especially after the Olympics. Now her family members, including grandparents, help her to answer fan mail. But no one else signs for Shannon. If there's a signature on the photograph or letter, it's her signature.

Newspapers continued to feature articles about Shannon. *The Edmond Evening Sun, The Oklahoma Gazette,* and *The Daily Oklahoman* featured their heroine in articles such as "Edmond Flips Over Gymnast"; "Miller Silver Shines Bright"; "Miller Becomes Media Darling"; "It's Miller Time"; "State Senators Salute Local Olympian"; and "Shannon: Nation's Hero."

Shannon and Trent Dimas, the only U.S. male gymnast to medal (a gold for his horizontal bar routine) found themselves on the September/October 1992 cover of *USA Gymnastics* magazine. They also appeared on ABC television's *Good Morning America* program.

In the fall of 1992, a team of Olympic and world-champion gymnasts gave a series of exhibitions in twenty-three U.S. cities. Shannon, always a crowd-pleaser, became one of the most popular gymnasts on the tour.

Shannon began 1993 with her second sweep in an international competition. In March, 12,000 people at the Orlando Arena in Florida saw Shannon win the all-around and every event at the McDonald's American Cup. In the individual apparatus finals, Shannon led throughout the entire competition, although teammate Kerri Strug was close behind all the way. An extra incentive at this meet was that McDonald's paid $1,000 for each first place. Counting Shannon's three preliminary victories, she took home $8,000 for doing what she likes to do best. Shannon was especially pleased with her American Cup all-around title, because on her three previous attempts she had placed sixth once, and twice she came in third.

The next meet was very important to Shannon. Her goal, as always, was to hit all of her routines and just do her best. But the World Championships in Birmingham, England, would also give her a chance to show that she was indeed the best gymnast in the world.

A gala celebration opened the championships. The audience watched a spectacular display of lasers, followed by dance performances from different countries. During the intermission, the audience had an opportunity to mingle with the gymnasts, take their pictures, and get autographs.

In the preliminaries, out of ninety-seven women, Shannon placed first, Dominique Dawes placed third, and Kerri Strug was fifth. Obviously, the United States could be proud of its team. Sadly for Kerri, this world competition only allowed two finalists per nation, unlike the Olympics, which allows up to three all-around competitors from one country. In the all-around, Shannon performed a strong routine on the bars, putting her in second place. Next, her errors on the beam dropped her to fifth place. She literally bounced into third place after her floor exercise. In the final rotation, she executed two full-twisting Yurchenko vaults. Both vaults were beautifully done, and Shannon received a 9.775 and a 9.8. The 9.8, under the new Code of Points, meant it was perfect. Gina Gogean of

Romania needed a 9.812 on her floor exercise to pass Shannon and take the gold. She gave a brilliant performance, but scored a 9.8. Shannon won the world title by only 0.007 of a point!

She didn't stop there. In spite of an upset stomach during the individual apparatus finals, she won the gold on the uneven bars over teammate Dominique Dawes. On the floor, she won the gold over Gina Gogean. Shannon became the first American gymnast to ever win three gold medals in a world championship.

Shannon says she really likes getting to see the sights in the different countries where she competes. It's not always possible to do this, but in England, Steve Nunno hired a private guide to take him, his assistant coach Peggy Liddick, and his two star gymnasts on a tour of London.

Kerri Strug says they had a great time. "We went to most of the famous museums, churches, and to Buckingham Palace. We shopped for souvenirs, especially Shannon—she bought a whole bunch of presents for her friends and family,'' says Kerri.

Kerri says that when she and Shannon were teammates at the Olympics, Shannon seemed to keep pretty much to herself. At that time, Kerri was at Bela Karolyi's gym in Houston, Texas. When Kerri later transferred to Steve Nunno's gym, she and Shannon became good friends. Together they attended parties for various girls in their gym and sometimes went out to eat at places like the Spaghetti Warehouse. One time they got massages, even though they were kind of expensive. ''Shannon and I could laugh together if it was a really bad day,'' Kerri says.

Once home from England, the best gymnast in the world tried to settle down to catch up on her schoolwork. ''The discipline I've learned from gymnastics helps me in other areas of my life, like getting organized and getting school-work done,'' Shannon explains.

Soon after her return, Governor David Walters proclaimed April 23, 1993, ''Shannon Miller Appreciation Day'' in the State of Oklahoma. Practically every week, Shannon received news of another honor or award she'd won.

Other opportunities came along. Elite Sportswear commissioned her to assist in designing her own workout collection of leotards, workout shorts, T-shirts, and warm-up suits. Shannon, who loves fashion, accepted the offer right away. She gets to help select the fabrics and styles for the outfits. She designed, and Tessa drew, the "SM" logo stamped on each item of clothing.

After taking time to model for her workout collection, Shannon traveled to Los Angeles, California, for her next competition, the Hilton Challenge. There she led the U.S. team to a first-place victory over Belarus and Ukraine. When these countries were united as a team for the Soviet Union, they had a stranglehold on women's gymnastics. After the 1992 Olympics, they began competing as fifteen separate countries, causing their gymnastic programs to lose the depth they once had. Shannon scored an impressive 39.287 to win first place all-around. Dominique Dawes came in second with 38.90, and Ukrainian Tatiana Lysenko placed third, as she had in the world championships.

A week later, from July 30 to August 1, Shannon competed in the U.S. Olympic Festival held in San Antonio, Texas. On the first day, her uneven bar routine drew a 9.95 and her floor exercise earned a 9.90. The crowd responded to her performance with two standing ovations. In the audience, Shannon's grandparents, Charles and Mabel Lee Miller, and her other San Antonio relatives, were bursting with pride. Shannon won the all-around with a 39.375, and Kerri Strug followed with a 38.825. On the last day, a crowd of 14,500 watched Shannon win three final event golds and one silver. Her near flawless floor routine was a 9.975, the highest score of the competition.

Mabel Lee Miller is impressed that her granddaughter can be in the limelight one minute and act like nothing important has happened the next. She says, ''After the Olympic Festival, Shannon came here, put on her nightgown, and she and Troy snacked while they watched TV. She acts just like regular folks.

"We'll ask to see her medals, and she'll put them out on the table for us. We congratulate her and tell her how proud we are. She smiles, and that's about it," Mrs. Miller says.

Shannon says, "One of the most exciting days in 1993 came for me when I won the all-around USA National Championship. Winning this event had been a goal of mine for a long time." Due to her injury in 1992, she had only competed in the compulsories.

Steve Nunno jokes about the order in which Shannon won her titles. "We did things in reverse order," he says. "First, she won five medals in the Olympic Games. Then she won the all-around and two events in the world championships, and, finally, she won the all-around title at the national championships."

The National Championship took place in Salt Lake City, Utah. Shannon was in great shape and felt optimistic about "hitting every one of her routines." She definitely did! She took first place in every event in the compulsories, posting the highest score in the competition on the bars, a 9.825. She continued into the

Tessa, six, and Shannon, four, with baby brother, Troy

(Olan Mills: The Nation's Studio)

Shannon at five
(Courtesy of the Miller family)

Tessa, ten, and Shannon, eight, perform the "Y" pose

(Courtesy of the Miller family)

Shannon, nearly twelve, at
the Dragon Invitational

(© Nancy Raymond /
International Gymnast*)*

1991 U. S. Classic

(© Nancy Raymond /
International Gymnast*)*

1991 World
Championships floor final

(© Nancy Raymond /
International Gymnast*)*

Getting last-minute
pointers from
Coach Nunno at the
1992 Olympics

(© Nancy Raymond /
International Gymnast*)*

1992 Olympics,
floor exercise ending pose

(© Nancy Raymond /
International Gymnast)

1992 Olympics,
mounting the balance beam
(Courtesy of Jerry Butler)

USA's 1992 Olympic bronze medal team
*(© Nancy Raymond /*International Gymnast*)*

Edmond's homecoming parade for Shannon after the Olympics

(Courtesy of the Miller family)

Shannon with coaches Peggy Liddick and Steve Nunno
and 1993 World Championship medals

Tatiana Gutsu (left) and Shannon on tour

(Courtesy of the Miller family)

1994 World
Championships

(© Nancy Raymond /
International Gymnast*)*

Shannon and her parents

(© Septima Green)

Shannon in her
senior year at
Edmond North High

*(Garrison's Photography;
Edmond, Oklahoma)*

optional phase of the competition, winning each event, and again making the highest score in the competition with a 9.90 on bars.

During individual apparatus finals, Shannon took first place on the bars and floor exercise, second place on the vault, and third place on the beam. On the balance beam, Shannon performed her own trick. She had introduced a new move at the world championships. The ''Miller'' is a back handspring, quarter turn, with a half hop. Only the best gymnasts get to have a movement named for them, so naturally Shannon felt happy and proud.

Atlanta, Georgia, hosted the Peachtree International Meet in early 1994, and Shannon won the all-around title plus three other golds and a silver medal for individual apparatus events.

The 1994 World Championships took place April 19–24 in Brisbane, Australia. This time, Shannon would be competing as the *defending* champion. No gymnast had retained a world title since Ludmilla Tourischeva of the Soviet Union twenty years before.

Shannon entered the competition cautiously.

She recently had recovered from a torn stomach muscle and nearly had to withdraw because of it. The crowd in the "Land Down Under" saw the all-around title come down to a close contest between Shannon and Romanian Lavinia Milosovici. Shannon came out on top by a 0.038 of a point!

Much to Shannon's satisfaction, she won a gold medal in the event finals for her beam performance. In the 1993 Worlds, she fell on the beam three times. Now, she had a world championship gold medal in every event except the vault.

Before the U.S. team left Australia, they did a little sight-seeing. Shannon's favorite activity was petting kangaroos and koalas.

In June, the U.S. gymnasts met the Romanian gymnasts in Worcester, Massachusetts, for the Budget Rent-a-Car Invitational. The Romanians were ready to reclaim their dominance over the United States. Their teams did win, and their male gymnast, Marius Urzica, won. But Shannon beat Gina Gogean, keeping the Romanians from having a sweep.

For two years after Barcelona, Shannon Miller was unbeatable. Her popularity was at an all-time high, and she seemed on top of the world in every area of her life.

8

Excellence at
Edmond North High

Shannon definitely was on top of the academic world. A member of the National Honor Society for four years, she made only one B in her high school career; all her other grades were As.

Regarding her education, she says, "School has always been important. I had the chance to do home schooling, but I wanted to stay in public schools. I can't put all my eggs in one basket, as they say, and just rely on gymnastics. I could sprain my ankle on the day of the Olympics and have missed all that school for nothing. I have to think of life after gymnastics as well."

Charles Woodham became principal of Edmond North in January 1993, and he recalls his first meeting with Shannon. "I was out in the hall around eight-fifteen one morning when Shannon came in from gymnastics practice. She was petite and carrying her book bag and books. Her book bag almost swallowed her up. I said 'hello' and introduced myself. She struck me as being somewhat shy. I think she endeared herself to the teachers because she studied, did all of her homework, and was a very determined young lady. She didn't need any pampering. Shannon was just Shannon."

Mr. Woodham says that since Shannon was gone so much and had a tutor, the state of Oklahoma approved a gifted and talented Individual Education Plan for her.

Terri Thomas, Shannon's tutor for three years, worked directly with the teachers to help Shannon complete her assignments. Terri says, "Shannon puts in as much time as it takes to do her work perfectly, not just to get it done."

In addition to helping Shannon with lessons, Terri sometimes travels with her when one of her parents can't go. Terri, Dynamo Gymnastics' account director, assumes a number of responsibilities at the gym. Away from the gym, she and Shannon are good friends and enjoy watching a rented movie or shopping together.

"One Saturday in November [of Shannon's sophomore year], we were sitting on the sofa studying. It was pouring rain, but Troy heard a squeaking noise from the backyard," Terri says. "Claudia went to see about it and found this little newborn puppy!" Tessa's dog, Ebony, had had three puppies. Shannon fed the puppy with an eyedropper and wanted to name him Dusty. She begged her parents to let her keep the pup, and they agreed. Ebony is part Labrador and part German shepherd. Because of Dusty's features and light yellow color, the Millers think his father must have been a golden retriever.

Shannon gives her dog a lot of love and attention. They walk or run together in the neighborhood where Shannon lives. Occasionally Dusty goes with the Millers to meet Shannon at the airport. Once she took Dusty to have his picture taken with Santa Claus. Jabba, one of Ebony's other pups, now belongs to Shannon's coach, Peggy Liddick.

The Millers also have two cats. Gizmo, a chunky gray male, has been around for a number of years. And in 1994, Troy adopted a fluffy, light-gray kitten that he named Carmen. Dusty, though, is the only animal allowed in Shannon's room.

Her small bedroom, decorated in peach and grayish blue colors, houses an assortment of stuffed animals, trophies, and gifts from fans. She says, "I'm a major pack rat. I keep everything!" In one corner, a hanging fish net holds 200 little stuffed animals. Most of her friends have given her a teddy bear at one time or another, and a lot of her fans send them. On either side of her single bed, she has built-in bookshelves containing souvenirs she's bought in the many countries she's visited, plus some of her trophies. At the foot of her bed, she has a hope chest containing many T-shirts from various trips or competitions and other keepsakes.

A coatrack on one wall says, "Shannon Miller's Gold Medal." A fan sent it after she narrowly missed getting the gold all-around at the Olympics. Some kids have sent her gold medals *they* have won! Another wall has pictures of the ocean and a sea bird that a twelve-year-old boy from California drew and sent as a gift. It's obvious that Shannon has thousands of adoring fans. She sincerely appreciates each of them and says she wishes she had more time to personalize responses for them.

Shannon has her own TV and VCR in her bedroom. She records reruns of *Cheers* and *Roseanne* plus one of her current favorite shows, *Friends*. She doesn't record any of her televised gymnastic meets and doesn't care to watch them. She explains, "I'd rather *do* gymnastics than watch it." Shannon reads or does homework in her room with the TV going but with the sound muted. She says, "I want some movement, even if it is in my peripheral vision, because it keeps me awake."

Judi Shortt, Shannon's sophomore honors English teacher, remembers the time they were doing a unit on *King Arthur*. She says, "For the grand finale, we had a big feast that took place in the library. Shannon and Kim Henry were the court jesters. They entertained us by doing acrobatic routines. It gave Shannon's classmates a chance to see her perform in person, which was good, because a lot of them hadn't seen her perform live.''

All of Shannon's teachers marvel at how conscientious she was about her schoolwork.

"We had lots of novels to read,'' says English teacher Ann Rutherford. "As my class ended, her next class was nearby, so in the six minutes between classes, she would read whatever novel we were on. She took advantage of the smallest amount of time.''

"She has a philosophy about going about things in a very organized way, and it's like gymnastics,'' says another former teacher, Joe Bosworth. "She does the same thing each day and never puts off things.''

Shannon's positive approach to learning paid off when she won the prestigious Dial Award. Each year two seniors are chosen by a nationwide panel who base their votes on athletic, academic, and civic accomplishment. The seniors receive their awards and a $5,000 grant for their high school at a dinner in Washington, D.C.

On May 18, 1995, Edmond North High School graduated 428 students in its first graduating class. Charles Woodham recalls, ''When Shannon walked up to receive her diploma, Superintendent Randall Raburn was so excited that he jumped out of his seat and presented it himself.'' Shannon's excellence at school had won the hearts of the administrators, faculty, and student body.

9

Shannon Serves
the Community

Perhaps the core of Shannon's excellence is her generous spirit. The people who know her have expressed it in many ways. Terri Thomas says, "My favorite part about Shannon is that she has such a big heart and is a really good person."

Near the end of her senior year, Shannon took time from her busy schedule to help her sophomore geometry teacher. Darrell Allen suffered from leukemia. The chemotherapy and other treatments he needed in his battle with cancer were more than his family could afford. Earlier in the year, Edmond North High had a fund-raiser for him, but Shannon was on a gymnastics trip. She wanted to think of a way to help her former teacher. She discussed it with her parents, and together they came up with the idea of a celebrity auction.

Shannon called her superstar athletic friends. She told them about her teacher and asked them to please donate items for the auction. Shaquille O'Neal, Nolan Ryan, Brian Boitano, Oksana Baiul, Bonnie Blair, Steffi Graf, Dan Jansen, Trent Dimas, Florence Griffith-Joyner, Bart Conner, Nadia Comaneci, and others sent auto-graphed and personal items. The auction, held Saturday, May 20, at the Dynamo Gym in Ed-mond, featured an exhibition from Dynamo's elite gymnasts. They charged one dollar admission. After the exhibition, Shannon and her group assisted participants with their bids. The auction netted $4,900 for the Allen family.

One of Shannon's priority charities is the Oklahoma Red Ribbon Campaign. As spokes-person for the organization, Shannon encourages young people to be drug free. She wears the

"Drug Free and Proud" sweatshirt for posters and makes statements in support of the activities that take place in almost every school across the state. Shannon says to young people, "I pledge that I will wear our 'Drug Free and Proud' Red Ribbon with pride as a youth, student, daughter, sister, Olympian, Oklahoman, and American." In her daily life, she models the importance of good health and staying drug free.

Shannon supports the Children's Miracle Network Telethon and serves as a local celebrity in Oklahoma. The money raised in Oklahoma is used statewide for children's hospitals. Shannon goes to the hospitals and spends time with the children. Before she leaves, the kids often want her autograph as a souvenir of the time they spent together. When she was in Atlanta, Georgia, in 1995, the United States Olympic Committee asked Shannon to visit kids at Egleston Children's Hospital at Emory University. People saw the way Shannon related to the young patients and were impressed. Shannon also supports the Make a Wish Foundation, Stay in

School, Alzheimer's Walk, and the American Lung Association.

Since Shannon makes time to give back to her community and other worthwhile programs, it's easy to see why, in 1994, the Rotary Club in Tulsa, Oklahoma, made her the first female recipient of the Henry P. Iba Citizen Award. In addition to a trophy, she received a $5,000 donation to be given to her favorite charity.

Edmond, Oklahoma, recognizes Shannon's charitable contributions. Because of these and the prominence she's brought to their city, they want to honor her. In 1995, two groups began their planning. The Shannon Miller Advisory Committee wants to place a bronze statue of her in Liberty Park. The statue will be located in a quiet area of town, near the library and some churches, and surrounded by large trees.

The Edmond Kiwanis Club plans to repaint a water tower at Interstate 35 and Second Street with Shannon's name. Both organizations hope to have their tributes completed before Shannon heads to Atlanta in July 1996.

10

Going for Gold in Atlanta

"*The most important thing in the Olympic Games is not to win but to take part, just as the most important thing in life is not the triumph but the struggle. The essential thing is not to have conquered but to have fought well.*"

This statement—the official creed for the modern Olympic Games—was written by Baron de Coubertin. However, it easily could have been written by Shannon Miller. It mirrors her philosophy. Whether she places first, second, or twentieth, she is there to do her best. The act of competition challenges and satisfies her.

Before Shannon goes to Atlanta, five things

69

have to happen. The first one has happened already. The U.S. women's gymnastics team had to *qualify* to compete at the Games at the 1995 World Championships in Sabae, Japan. The twelve top-scoring countries get to compete in Atlanta. The United States team placed third.

Next, gymnasts compete in the 1996 USA National Championships in Knoxville, Tennessee, on June 5–8. There, the national teams will be announced. Even if a girl already is on the team, she has to requalify each year. In 1990, at age thirteen, Shannon became the youngest member to ever join the U.S. senior national team. She has qualified every year since.

Then, top members from the U.S. national team earn the right to compete at the Olympic Trials in Boston, Massachusetts, on June 27–30. The scores a girl makes at the trials combine with the ones she made at the nationals to determine whether she is selected for the squad. After the trials, the athletes are hastened off to training camp to practice and polish their routines.

Finally, the lucky seven (six members and

one alternate) who officially make the Olympic team will go through processing for the 1996 Olympic Games in Atlanta, Georgia.

Women's gymnastics is *the* most popular sport of all the summer Olympic Games. All tickets to gymnastics events were sold a year before the 1996 Games. Next to the Opening Ceremonies, the United States Olympic Committee had more ticket requests for the women's gymnastics all-around than any other event. In the top eight Olympic event sell-outs, all five women's gymnastics events were included!

Shannon attended Oklahoma University only part time in 1995–96 to allow herself more time to concentrate on routines for the Olympics. Regarding a college major, she says, "Nothing is set in stone. Right now, I'm a business major because it covers a broad area. The six hours I'm taking are psychology and world regional geography." She explains that those subjects were the only ones left when she registered at Oklahoma University. She still lives at home, but after the Olympics, she plans to go away to college.

Before enrolling in college, Shannon had to fulfill a contract she had made with USA Team Gymnastics Camp. Coach Peggy Liddick accompanied her to New York. "Shannon smiles, greets the campers, poses for pictures, and signs autographs. The campers love her!" Peggy says.

"After Shannon made her camp appearances, we spent the weekend in New York City," Peggy continues. "We went to *Phantom of the Opera* on Broadway. Shannon's mouth was open while she was watching. She was so appreciative of the actors' talent. She exclaimed, 'Gosh, it must be nice to be so talented!' She watched the whole play, never taking her eyes off the performance."

Peggy says she and Shannon went shopping in downtown New York. "Nobody recognized us. It was great! We tried on hats, being silly. And we bargained with the street vendors."

For lunch, they went to the Waldorf-Astoria hotel restaurant. Shannon ordered a plain turkey croissant sandwich. Even in a nice restaurant, she sticks to her healthy diet.

After the New York trip, it was back to Oklahoma, back to the real world, and back to training. At the 1995 Nationals, held in New Orleans, Louisiana, August 16–19, Shannon sought to reclaim the Nationals title that Dominique Dawes took in 1994. Instead of either of the two previous title holders recapturing the top national position, a young, up-and-coming gymnast, Dominique Moceanu, claimed it. One month shy of being fourteen, Dominique became the youngest person to accomplish this feat. If Shannon hadn't fallen on the balance beam and received a 0.5 deduction, she would have gotten the all-around. Instead, she had to settle for second place again.

But not in the individual event finals! Shannon took first place on the vault, Dominique Dawes won on bars and floor, and Doni Thompson and Monica Flammer tied for first on the beam. Shannon also took third place for her floor exercise.

Three weeks later at the World Trials in Austin, Texas, Shannon outscored Dominique Moceanu, but the weighted scoring of the USA

Nationals combined with the trials gave Dominique a slight edge.

In October at the World Championships, Shannon was third in the world (first in the United States) after compulsories. Unfortunately, she injured her right foot on a beam dismount. If she hadn't continued in the optional competition, the U.S. team would have lost the bronze medal to Russia.

In the all-around and individual event finals, she could barely walk. She knew she wouldn't be able to reclaim her title, but Shannon's favorite aspect of her sport is competing, so she was determined to finish the meet. She placed twelfth out of the thirty-six who had qualified for the all-around finals. In the individual event finals, only Ukraine's Lilia Podkopayeva, China's Mo Huilan, and Shannon qualified for all four events. Steve Nunno recommended that she cancel the vault and floor exercise because of her foot injury. She placed fourth on the beam and seventh on bars.

Although Shannon says there never has been a time when she thought of herself as ''a great gymnast," history and those who have seen her perform disagree. Shannon says, "I worked hard at it. I stuck with it. I've had great coaches. I went up in levels. And that's it."

When asked what she'd probably be doing in twenty years, she mused, "Well, in my late thirties, hopefully I'll be married. Maybe I'll have a kid or two. Hopefully I'll have a well-rounded life and a nice job. I'd like to still be in Oklahoma. I love it here."

Shannon doesn't worry about the future; she remains focused on her immediate goals. Right now, her goal is to make the Olympic team and help the United States win the team gold. U.S. gymnasts have more depth than they've ever had. Many speculate the U.S. team will be golden in Atlanta.

Will the United States flag be raised for Shannon at the 1996 Olympic Games? Will the now five feet, ninety-four pound Shannon gain a spot on the awards podium and add to her collection of Olympic medals? To find out, millions of fans around the world will be watching the graceful, elegant nineteen-year-old Shannon.

As for Shannon, her smile will be the same. She treats victory and defeat as equals. Because she does her best, she finds peace with the results of her efforts. Whatever happens in Atlanta, with five Olympic and nine World Championship medals, she already is the most decorated gymnast in American history.

Shannon's National Competitions

●

Year	Competition	Location	Team	AA*	Vault	Bars	Beam	Floor
1995	American Classic	Oakland, California	1	2	2		1	1
1994	Championships of the USA	Nashville, Tennessee	2	2	2		2	2
1993	Championships of the USA	Salt Lake City, Utah	1	2	1		3	1
1993	U.S. Olympic Sports Festival	San Antonio, Texas		1	1		1	1
1992	U.S. Olympic Trials	Baltimore, Maryland		1				
1992	Championships of the USA	Columbus, Ohio	1	(compulsories only)				
1991	World Championships Team Trials	Indianapolis, Indiana	3				1	6
1991	Championships of the USA	Cincinnati, Ohio	7	3			2	1
1991	U.S. Classic	Huntington Beach, California	2				1	1
1990	American Classic	Tempe, Arizona	2				1	1
1990	Championships of the USA	Denver, Colorado	8				6	5
1990	U.S. Classic	Saginaw, Michigan	2				2	1
1989	U.S. Olympic Sports Festival (Jr. A)	Oklahoma City, Oklahoma	3	2		1	5	6
1989	U.S. Classic (Jr. A)	San Antonio, Texas	6	5		7	1	3
1989	American Classic (Jr. A)	Oakland, California	1		1	1	1	1
1988	U.S. Classic (Jr. B)	Athens, Georgia	1	1		1	1	1
1988	American Classic (Jr. B)	Phoenix, Arizona	2		1	1	1	4

*AA = All-Around.

Shannon's International Competitions

			Team	AA*	Vault	Bars	Beam	Floor
1995	Pan American Games	Mar del Plata, Argentina	1	1	2	1		1
1995	McDonald's American Cup	Seattle, Washington		3			(Preliminaries)	
1994	World Team Championships	Dortmund, Germany	2					
1994	Goodwill Games	St. Petersburg, Russia	2	2	2	1		1
1994	USA-Romania, Budget Rent-a-Car	Worcester, Massachusetts	2	1				
1994	World Gymnastics Championships	Brisbane, Australia		1			1	
1994	Peachtree International Meet	Atlanta, Georgia		1	1	1	1	
1993	Hilton Challenge	Los Angeles, California	1	1				
1993	World Gymnastics Championships	Birmingham, England		1		1		1
1993	Reebok International Mixed Pairs	Atlanta, Georgia		4	(with Lance Ringnald)			
1993	McDonald's American Cup	Orlando, Florida		1	1		1	1
1992	Olympic Games	Barcelona, Spain	3	2	6	3	2	3
1992	McDonald's International Mixed Pairs	Tallahassee, Florida		1	(with Scott Keswick)			
1992	McDonald's American Cup	Orlando, Florida		3				
1991	DTB Pokal	Stuttgart, Germany		3	3	2		1

Year	Event	Location	Team	AA*	Vault	Bars	Beam	Floor
1991	Arthur Gander Memorial	Montreux, Switzerland		1	1	1	1	1
1991	Swiss Cup	St. Gallen, Switzerland		1	*(with Scott Keswick)*			
1991	World Gymnastics Championships	Indianapolis, Indiana	2	6	6	2	6	4
1991	USA vs. Romania	Houston, Texas	2	3	3		1	3
1991	McDonald's International Mixed Pairs	Atlanta, Georgia		9	*(with Patrick Kirksey)*			
1991	McDonald's American Cup	Orlando, Florida		3	(Preliminaries)			
1990	Catania Cup	Catania, Italy		1	1	2	1	1
1990	McDonald Challenge, USA vs USSR	San Jose, California		6				
1990	Pyramid Challenge, USA vs GDR	Memphis, Tennessee	1	7				
1990	Canadian Cup	Toronto, Canada		9				
1990	McDonald's International Mixed Pairs	Villanova, Pennsylvania		17	*(with Tom Schlesinger)*			
1990	McDonald's American Cup	Fairfax, Virginia		6	(Preliminaries)			
1989	International Junior Gymnastics Competition	Yokohama, Japan		6				
1988	Junior Pan-American Games	Ponce, Puerto Rico	1	2	2			3

*AA = All-Around.

Shannon's Awards and Honors

●

1994

1994 "Dial Award," National High School Athlete/Scholar—The Dial Corporation

Finalist for the 1994 "James E. Sullivan Award"—Amateur Athletic Union

1994 "Special Award," Oklahoma Sports Headliner Awards—March of Dimes

"Enrique Camarena" Award Nominee—National Family Partnership

1994 "Athlete of the Year" for Women's Artistic Gymnastics—the U.S. Olympic Committee

1994 "Woman Athlete of the Year"—USA Gymnastics

1994 "Presidential Medallion"—USA Gymnastics

1994 "Favorite Female Athlete"—Nomination, Kids' Choice Award—Nickelodeon

Finalist for the 1994 "Sportswoman of the Year"—Women's Sports Foundation

Finalist for the 1994 Babe Dedrickson Zaharias Award

1994 "Henry P. Iba Citizen Athlete Award"—Rotary Club of Tulsa, Oklahoma, the First Recipient

1994 U.S. Olympic Committee "Woman Athlete of the Month"—April

1993

Finalist for the 1993 "James E. Sullivan Award"—Amateur Athletic Union

1993 "Special Award," Oklahoma Sports Headliner Awards—March of Dimes

1993 "Athlete of the Year" for Women's Artistic Gymnastics—the U.S. Olympic Committee

International Finalist for the Jesse Owens Award

Finalist for the 1993 Babe Dedrickson Zaharias Award

1993 "Award of Distinction" for Gymnastics—Touchdown Club of Columbus, Ohio

"Master of Sport" Award—USA Gymnastics, Third woman ever to receive the award

1993 "Female Athlete of the Year"—National March of Dimes

1993 "Best Local Sports Figure"—The Oklahoma City Gazette Newspaper

April 26, Honorary County Commissioner of Oklahoma County

May 4, "Governor's Youth Award"—State of Oklahoma

1993 U.S. Olympic Committee "Woman Athlete of the Month"—April

1993 U.S. Olympic Committee "Woman Athlete of the Month"—March

April 23, 1993, proclaimed "Shannon Miller Appreciation Day" in the State of Oklahoma by the governor

1992

1992 "Steve Reeves Award"—New York Downtown Athletic Club, First woman recipient

1992 "Sports Headliner of the Year," Oklahoma Sports Headliner Awards—March of Dimes

1992 "Athlete of the Year" for Artistic Gymnastics—the U.S. Olympic Committee

Finalist for the 1992 Babe Dedrickson Zaharias Award

1992 "Kids Choice Award"—Nickelodeon

1992 "Women's Gymnast of the Year"—Touchdown Club of Columbus, Ohio

1992 "Edmond Citizen of the Year"—Edmond, Oklahoma Chamber of Commerce

1992 "Jim Thorpe Award"—Oklahoma AAU; first person ever presented

Nominated by the Oklahoma AAU for the 1992 Sullivan Award

"Oklahoma Ambassador of Goodwill," declaration by Governor David Walters

Honorary Lieutenant Governor of the State of Oklahoma

Honorary Mayor of Oklahoma City: July 2, 1992

July 2, 1992, declared "Shannon Lee Miller Day" in the State of Oklahoma by Governor David Walters

1992 "NUPRIN Comeback Award" honoring a female Olympic athlete who overcame injury

"Evian Performance Award" for her outstanding effort in winning the 1992 USA Olympic Trials

1991

1991 "Up & Coming Award"—Women's Sports Foundation

Useful Addresses

●

USA Gymnastics Office
and *USA Gymnastics* magazine
201 South Capital Avenue
Indianapolis, Indiana 46225

International Gymnast magazine
P.O. Box 721020
Norman, Oklahoma 73070

Gym Stars magazine
44 Fitzjohn's Avenue
London NW3 5LX
England

Gymnastics Hall of Fame
227 Brooks Street
Oceanside, California 92054

United States Olympic Committee
1 Olympic Plaza
Colorado Springs, Colorado 80909

President's Council on Physical Fitness
701 Pennsylvania Avenue, NW, Suite 250
Washington, D.C. 20004